# Mothers

by Lola M. Schaefer

Consulting Editor: Gail Saunders-Smith, Ph.D.

Consultant: Phyllis Edelbrock, First-Grade Teacher,
University Place School District, Washington

## Pebble Books

an imprint of Capstone Press
Mankato, Minnesota

Pebble Books are published by Capstone Press
151 Good Counsel Drive, P.O. Box 669, Mankato, Minnesota 56002
http://www.capstone-press.com

2  3  4  5  6  7  07  06  05  04  03  02

*Library of Congress Cataloging-in-Publication Data*
Schaefer, Lola M., 1950–
    Mothers / by Lola M. Schaefer.
    p. cm.—(Families)
    Summary: Simple text and photographs depict mothers and what they do with
their children.
    ISBN 0-7368-0259-2 (hardcover)
    ISBN 0-7368-4840-1 (paperback)
    1. Mothers—Juvenile literature. 2. Mother and child—Juvenile literature. [1.
Mothers. Mother and child.] I. Title.  II. Series: Schaefer, Lola M., 1950- Families.
    HQ759.S2735  1999
    306.874′3—dc21                                                          98-31600

# Note to Parents and Teachers

The Family series supports national social studies standards for units related to identifying family members and their roles in the family. This book describes and illustrates mothers and activities they do with their children. The photographs support emergent readers in understanding the text. The repetition of words and phrases helps emergent readers learn new words. This book also introduces emergent readers to subject-specific vocabulary words, which are defined in the Words to Know section. Emergent readers may need assistance to read some words and to use the Table of Contents, Words to Know, Read More, Internet Sites, and Index/Word List sections of the book.

# Table of Contents

A mother is a female parent.

Mothers fix bikes.

8

Mothers wash cars.

Mothers visit school.

Mothers play golf.

14

Mothers blow up balloons.

Mothers skate.

Mothers laugh.

Mothers love.

# Words to Know

**female**—a girl or woman; mothers are females.

**golf**—a game in which players use special clubs to hit a small ball into holes on a course

**laugh**—to make a sound that shows you think something is funny

**love**—to like someone or something very much

**skate**—to move along on skates

**wash**—to clean with water or soap and water

# Read More

**Kaplan, John.** *Mom and Me.* New York: Scholastic, 1996.

**Morris, Ann.** *The Mommy Book.* The World's Family. Parsippany, N.J.: Silver Press, 1996.

**Saunders-Smith, Gail.** *Parents.* People. Mankato, Minn.: Pebble Books, 1998.

# Internet Sites

**Happy Mother's Day!**
http://headlines.yahoo.com/Full_Coverage/
Yahooligans/Celebrate_Moms

**A History of Mother's Day**
http://www.chron.com/content/interactive/special/
holidays/97/mom/history.html

**Mother's Day Celebration**
http://www.agirlsworld.com/amy/pajama/
mothersday/index.html

23

# Index/Word List

balloons, 15
bikes, 7
blow up, 15
cars, 9
female, 5
fix, 7
golf, 13
laugh, 19
love, 21

mother, 5, 7, 9, 11,
  13, 15, 17, 19, 21
parent, 5
play, 13
school, 11
skate, 17
visit, 11
wash, 9

**Word Count: 28**
**Early-Intervention Level: 5**

**Editorial Credits**
Mari C. Schuh, editor; Steve Weil/Tandem Design, cover designer and illustrator;
    Kimberly Danger, photo researcher

**Photo Credits**
David F. Clobes, 18
International Stock/Laurie Bayer, 12
Mark Turner, 6, 8, 14
PhotoBank, Inc./Don Romero, cover; Bill Lai, 1, 4; Ted Wilcox, 16
Shaffer Photography/James L. Shaffer, 10
Transparencies, Inc./Tom McCarthy, 20

Special thanks to Joy Allison, Lori Hollenback, and Penny McCarthy, first-grade
teachers at Evergreen Primary in University Place, Washington, for reviewing the
books in the Families series.